More Than Just A Payout

More Than Just A Payout

How Life Insurance Builds Security and Opportunity

Ramoth Watson

More Than Just A Payout: How Life Insurance Builds Security and Opportunity

Copyright © 2025 Ramoth Watson

All rights reserved.

Contact the Author:
Ramoth Watson
ramothwatson@gmail.com
IG: @ramoth1
Facebook: Ramoth Watson

Publishing Support by:
The Self-Publish Connection
Kingston, Jamaica
https://theselfpublishconnection.com

ISBN: **978-976-655-167-4**

Dedication

To the individuals, families, professionals, business owners, and students who are committed to protecting their loved ones and securing their financial future.

This book is for those who seek not just knowledge but confidence and clarity in their financial journey. It is for lifelong learners, planners, dreamers, and doers. Those who understand that financial security is not just about numbers on a page, but about peace of mind, freedom, and the ability to shape a future filled with opportunities.

May these pages empower you to make informed decisions that go beyond mere protection, helping you build lasting wealth, security, and a meaningful legacy. May they serve as a guide, a source of inspiration, and a reminder that every step you take today has the power to shape your future and that of those you love.

To your journey of wisdom, prosperity, and purpose, this book is dedicated to you.

Table of Contents

Preface

Life insurance is often misunderstood; many view it as an unnecessary or overly complicated product. After 34 years in the industry, I have witnessed firsthand how the right policy can shield families from financial hardship and provide lasting security.

I wrote this book to demystify life insurance and empower you to make informed decisions for your future. Whether you are new to life insurance or looking to fine-tune your existing coverage, this guide offers clear, practical advice to help you protect what matters most.

Introduction: Life Insurance - More Than Just a Payout

Most people think of life insurance as a means to provide financial support to loved ones after they're gone. While that's true, it's only part of the story. Life insurance isn't just about death; it's about financial empowerment, security, and opportunity.

Imagine a financial tool that can:

- Replace lost income so your family doesn't struggle.
- Pay off debts so loved ones aren't left with financial burdens.
- Fund a child's education or create an inheritance.
- Act as an investment vehicle, accumulating cash value over time.
- Support your business or retirement with tax-advantaged benefits.
- Manage complex relationships in blended families and support your philanthropic legacy.

Yet, despite these benefits, many people hesitate to get coverage. Some think it's too expensive, complicated, or unnecessary. Others assume their employer-provided insurance is enough until they realize it may not fully cover their needs.

This book is here to break down life insurance simply and practically. Whether you're a young professional, a parent, a business owner, or a student planning for the future, you'll learn:

- What types of policies exist, and which one is right for you?
- How much coverage do you really need? (Hint: It's probably more than you think.)
- Ways to use life insurance while you're still alive, from borrowing against cash value to funding a legacy.
- Common mistakes to avoid when choosing a policy.

Life insurance isn't just about preparing for the worst; it's about making the most of life today. Let's dive in and uncover how life insurance can work for you.

Chapter 1: The Basics of Life Insurance

Life insurance is one of the most important financial tools available, yet it remains misunderstood by many. Some see it as just an expense, others as a safety net only for those with dependents. But the truth is, life insurance is more than just a death benefit; it's a financial plan that protects you and your loved ones both now and in the future.

This chapter will break down the basics of life insurance, including who needs it and how it works, so you can confidently take the next step toward securing your financial future.

What Is Life Insurance?

At its core, life insurance is a contract between you and an insurance company. In exchange for regular premium payments, the insurer promises to pay a death benefit to your designated beneficiaries when you pass away.

But life insurance isn't just about covering funeral costs; it can also:
- Provide income replacement for your family.
- Pay off debts like mortgages, student loans, and credit cards.
- Fund long-term goals such as your child's education.
- Support your business or estate planning needs.

Life insurance can also be used while you're alive, depending on the type of policy you choose. Some policies build cash value, which can be borrowed against, withdrawn, or used to supplement retirement income.

Who Needs Life Insurance?

Many assume life insurance is only for those with families, but it's useful for almost everyone. If anyone depends on your income or would struggle financially after your passing, you likely need coverage.

Here are some groups that benefit from life insurance:

Individuals & Young Professionals

- A policy can cover outstanding debts, such as student loans or medical bills, even if you're single with no dependents.
- Buying early locks with lower premiums while you're young and healthy.

Families & Parents

- Provides financial security for children, spouses, and dependents.
- It can help cover day-to-day living expenses, childcare, and future education costs.

✅ Business Owners & Entrepreneurs

- Ensures continuity in case a key business partner or owner passes away.
- It can be used in buy-sell agreements to protect company ownership.

✅ Students & Recent Graduates

- It helps cover private student loan debt, which doesn't always disappear after death.
- Offers an opportunity to lock in low rates before potential health issues arise.

✅ Retirees & Estate Planners

- It helps cover estate taxes and final expenses to avoid burdening loved ones.
- It can be used for legacy planning or charitable giving.

What is the bottom line? If someone depends on you, whether it's financially, emotionally, or for business stability, you need life insurance.

The Psychological Benefits of Life Insurance

Beyond financial considerations, life insurance offers peace of mind. Knowing that your family or business won't struggle financially if something happens to you brings a priceless level of security.

1. **Reduces Anxiety** – Many worry about what would happen to their loved ones if they weren't around. A policy eliminates that fear.

2. **Encourages Better Financial Planning** – Having life insurance often leads to more responsible budgeting, investing, and saving.

3. **Allows You to Enjoy the Present** – Instead of stressing over "what ifs," you can focus on living life fully, knowing your financial safety net is in place.

How Life Insurance Works

Getting life insurance is a simple process, but understanding how it works ensures you choose the right policy for your needs. Here's an overview of the key components:

1. **<u>The Application Process</u>**

   - You choose a policy type and coverage amount based on your needs.
   - You complete an application, answering questions about your health, lifestyle, and finances.

- Some policies require a medical exam, while others offer no-exam options at a higher cost.

2 <u>Underwriting & Approval</u>

- The insurance company evaluates your risk level (age, health, occupation, etc.).
- Premiums are determined based on this assessment.
- Once approved, you begin making regular payments (premiums).

3 <u>Paying Premiums & Maintaining Your Policy</u>

- You can pay premiums monthly, quarterly, semi-annually or annually.
- Missing payments could lapse your policy, meaning you'd lose coverage.

4 <u>The Claims Process & Payout</u>

- Beneficiaries file a claim with the insurance company when the policyholder passes away.
- Once approved, the death benefit is paid out as a lump sum or a structured payment.

Final Thoughts: The Foundation of Financial Security

Life insurance is more than just a financial tool; it's a commitment to securing the future of those you love. Whether you're looking for simple coverage or a policy that builds wealth, understanding the basics is the first step toward making an informed decision.

In the next chapter, we'll explore the different types of life insurance, allowing you to determine which policy best suits your needs.

Chapter 2: Types of Life Insurance Policies

Not all life insurance policies are the same. Choosing the right one depends on your financial goals, budget, and coverage needs. In this chapter, we'll break down the major types of life insurance so you can make an informed decision.

The Two Main Categories of Life Insurance

All life insurance policies fall into one of two main categories:

- Term Life Insurance – Coverage for a specific period (e.g., 10, 20, or 30 years). It is typically the most affordable option.

- Permanent Life Insurance – Provides lifetime coverage and includes a savings component (cash value) that grows over time.

Let's explore each in detail.

Section 1: Term Life Insurance

What Is Term Life Insurance?

Term life insurance provides coverage for a set number of years, such as 10, 20, or 30 years. If you pass away during this time, your beneficiaries receive a death benefit. If you outlive the term, the policy expires with no payout (unless you renew or convert it).

Pros of Term Life Insurance

- ☑ Lower cost – It's the most affordable life insurance option.
- ☑ Straightforward coverage – No investment components, just a pure death benefit.
- ☑ Good for short-term needs – Ideal for protecting young families, paying off a mortgage, or covering income replacement for a specific period.

Cons of Term Life Insurance

- ☒ Temporary coverage – If you outlive the policy, there's no payout.
- ☒ Premiums increase upon renewal – If you want to extend coverage later in life, it may become expensive.
- ☒ No cash value accumulation – Unlike permanent life insurance, it does not accumulate cash value.

Who Should Consider Term Life Insurance?

- Young families who want affordable coverage while raising children.
- Homeowners with a mortgage to protect.
- Individuals who need temporary financial protection (e.g., until retirement).

Section 2: Permanent Life Insurance

What Is Permanent Life Insurance?

Unlike term life, permanent life insurance lasts your entire life (as long as you pay your premiums). It also includes a cash value component, which grows over time and can be used while you're alive.

Types of Permanent Life Insurance

There are various types of permanent life insurance policies, each offering distinct benefits.

1 Whole Life Insurance

- Provides fixed premiums and guaranteed lifetime coverage.
- Cash value grows at a guaranteed rate.
- It can be used for estate planning or wealth transfer.

 Best for those who want predictability and long-term security.

2 Universal Life Insurance

- More flexible than whole life; you can adjust premiums and death benefits.
- The cash value earns interest based on market rates.
- Some policies allow loans or withdrawals from the cash value.

 Ideal for those seeking flexibility and opportunities for growth.

3 Variable Life Insurance

- Combines life insurance with investment options (stocks, bonds, etc.).
- Higher growth potential but also higher risk.
- Cash value fluctuates based on investment performance.

 Best suited for individuals who are comfortable with investment risk.

Pros of Permanent Life Insurance

☑ Lifelong coverage – No need to renew or reapply.

☑ Cash value grows over time – Acts as a savings or investment tool.

☑ It can be utilized for wealth transfer and estate planning purposes.

Cons of Permanent Life Insurance

☒ Higher cost – More expensive than term life.

☒ It can be complex, requiring an understanding of fees, growth potential, and tax implications.

☒ Not always necessary – Some people only need coverage for a specific period, making term life a better fit.

Section 3: Comparing Term vs. Permanent Life Insurance

Feature	Term Life Insurance	Permanent Life Insurance
Coverage Duration	Fixed term (e.g., 10, 20, 30 years)	Lifetime coverage
Cost	Lower premiums	Higher premiums
Cash Value	☒ No cash value	☑ Builds cash value over time
Best For	Short-term financial needs	Long-term financial security and estate planning
Flexibility	Cannot be modified after purchase	Some policies allow premium/death benefit adjustments

The best policy depends on your financial goals, budget, and the duration of coverage you require.

Section 4: Hybrid and Special Policies

Some policies combine aspects of term and permanent insurance or provide unique benefits:

Convertible Term Life Insurance

- It starts as term life but can be converted to permanent insurance without a medical exam.
- Ideal for those who want affordable coverage now but may need lifelong coverage later.

Return of Premium (ROP) Term Life Insurance

- If you outlive the policy, your premiums will be refunded.
- Higher cost than regular term life, but offers some financial return.

Final Expense Insurance (Burial Insurance)

- A whole-life policy designed to cover funeral costs and final expenses.
- No medical exam is required, which makes it easier for seniors to qualify.

Final Thoughts: Choosing the Right Policy

Now that you understand the different types of life insurance, the next step is to determine which one fits your needs best. If you need affordable, temporary protection, term life may be your best choice. A permanent policy may be better if you want lifelong security and cash value benefits.

In the next chapter, we'll explore how life insurance policies work, including underwriting, premium payments, and what happens when a claim is filed.

Chapter 3: How Life Insurance Works

Now that you understand the different types of life insurance, let's dive into how these policies actually work, from application to payouts. Whether you're buying a policy or ensuring your loved ones know how to claim benefits, this chapter will clarify every step.

Section 1: The Life Insurance Process

1 **Applying for a Policy**

When you apply for life insurance, the insurer assesses your risk before issuing coverage. The application process generally includes:

- Personal Information – Age, occupation, income, and lifestyle.
- Health Information – Medical history, pre-existing conditions, and sometimes a medical exam.
- Policy Details – Type of policy, coverage amount, and beneficiaries.

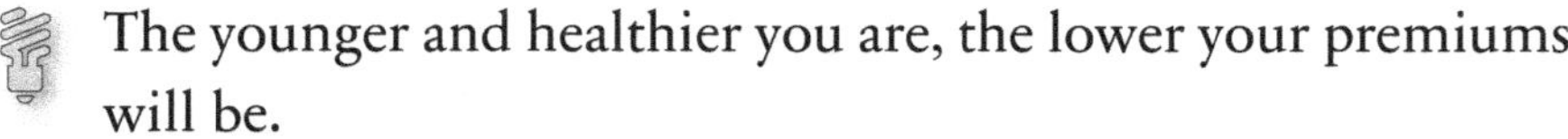 The younger and healthier you are, the lower your premiums will be.

② Understanding Underwriting & Risk Assessment

Underwriting is the process insurers use to evaluate how risky you are to insure. They look at factors such as:

- Age – Younger applicants typically get lower rates.
- Health History – Chronic conditions can increase premiums.
- Family Medical History – Hereditary illnesses may impact eligibility.
- Lifestyle Choices – Smoking, alcohol use, and dangerous hobbies (e.g., skydiving) can result in higher rates.
- Occupation – Risky jobs (firefighters, pilots, construction workers) may require higher premiums.

After reviewing these factors, insurers categorize applicants into risk categories, which in turn affect pricing.

Risk Category	Description	Effect on Premiums
Preferred Plus	Excellent health, no risk factors	Lowest premiums
Preferred	Good health, minor risk factors	Low premiums
Standard	Average health, manageable risks	Moderate premiums
Substandard	Significant health or lifestyle risks	Higher premiums or possible denial

 Even if you have health issues, some insurers offer simplified or guaranteed issue policies that do not require medical exams (although these policies may come at a higher cost).

Section 2: Paying Premiums & Keeping Your Policy Active

Once your policy is approved, you must pay premiums regularly to maintain active coverage.

How Premiums Are Calculated

Your premium depends on:
- Age & Health – Younger, healthier people pay lower premiums.
- Policy Type – Term life is cheaper than permanent life.
- Coverage Amount – Higher death benefits mean higher premiums.
- Additional Riders – Extra features (e.g., disability waivers) increase costs.

Ways to Pay Premiums

Most insurers offer monthly, quarterly, semi-annual, or annual payments. Some policies also allow for:
- Automatic deductions from your bank account or salary for convenience.

- Flexible payments (in some permanent policies) where you can adjust premiums.

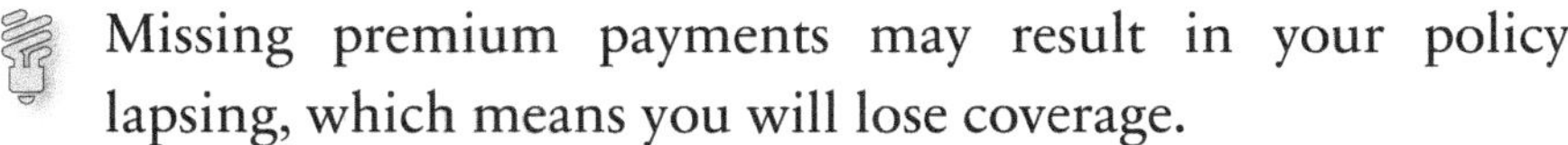 Missing premium payments may result in your policy lapsing, which means you will lose coverage.

Section 3: The Claims Process & How Beneficiaries Receive Payouts

If the policyholder passes away, the beneficiary must file a claim to receive the death benefit. Here's what happens next:

1 **Filing a Claim**

- Contact the insurance company.
- Submit a death certificate and policy details.
- Complete a claim form.

2 **How the Insurer Processes the Claim**

- The insurer reviews the policy terms and the cause of death.
- If there are no issues, the claim is approved.
- If there are concerns (e.g., the policyholder died within the contestability period), the insurer may investigate further.

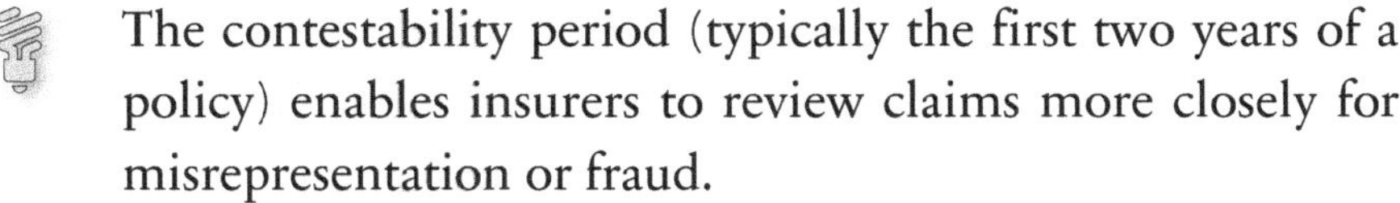 The contestability period (typically the first two years of a policy) enables insurers to review claims more closely for misrepresentation or fraud.

3 How Beneficiaries Receive Payout

Beneficiaries can usually choose how they want to receive the money:

- Lump Sum – A one-time payment of the entire death benefit.
- Installments/Annuity – The insurer pays out over time in regular payments.
- Retained Asset Account – The insurer holds the funds in an interest-bearing account until the beneficiary withdraws them.

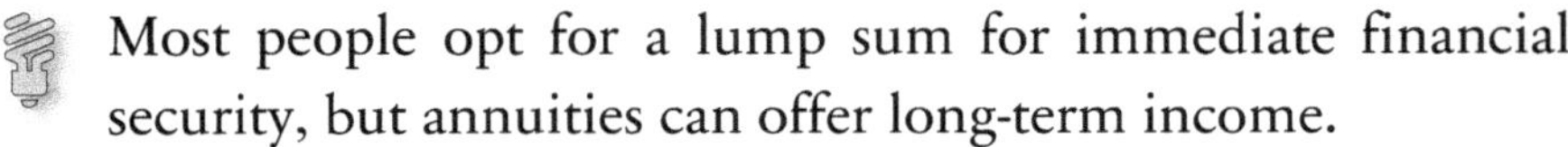 Most people opt for a lump sum for immediate financial security, but annuities can offer long-term income.

Section 4: What Happens If a Claim Is Denied?

Sometimes, insurers deny claims due to policy exclusions, misrepresentation, or lapses in coverage. Here's what to do if that happens:

Common Reasons for Denial

☒ Non-Disclosure of Health Issues – The claim may be denied if the policyholder fails to disclose a pre-existing medical condition.

☒ Policy Lapse – No payout will be made if premiums are not paid and the policy has expired.

☒ Contestability Period Issues – If the insured dies within the first 2 years and the insurer finds false information on the application, they may refuse to pay.

☒ Suicide Clause – Most policies won't pay if the policyholder dies by suicide within the first 1–2 years.

How to Appeal a Denied Claim

☑ Review the reason for denial – Request a formal explanation from the insurer.

☑ Provide additional documentation – Sometimes, medical records or other evidence can support your claim.

☑ Consult a lawyer or financial advisor – If you believe the denial was unfair, seeking legal assistance may be beneficial.

💡 Understanding your policy terms beforehand can help prevent issues later.

Final Thoughts: Understanding How Life Insurance Works

Life insurance is more than just a contract; it's a financial promise. Understanding the application process, premium payments, and claims process ensures that you and your loved ones will benefit fully from your policy.

Next, we'll delve into how to determine your ideal coverage amount, ensuring your loved ones are financially secure.

Chapter 4: Determining Your Coverage Needs

Choosing the right amount of life insurance is crucial. Too little coverage leaves your loved ones financially vulnerable, while too much may result in unnecessarily high premiums. This chapter will help you determine the right coverage amount based on your financial responsibilities, future goals, and personal circumstances.

Section 1: Why Coverage Amount Matters

Many people underestimate how much life insurance they need. They assume their savings, employer-provided coverage, or investments will be enough. However, without careful planning, their family may face:

- ☒ Loss of income – Surviving family members may struggle to cover day-to-day expenses.
- ☒ Outstanding debts – Mortgages, car loans, and student loans don't disappear.
- ☒ Education costs – If you plan to fund your child's college education, you need coverage to support it.
- ☒ Unforeseen expenses – Funeral costs, medical bills, and estate taxes can add up quickly.

 The right coverage provides peace of mind, ensuring your family maintains their lifestyle and financial security.

Section 2: The 3 Key Factors to Consider

When calculating your coverage needs, consider these three factors:

1 Income Replacement

- How many years would your family need financial support?
- A common rule of thumb is having coverage 10–15 times your annual income.
- If you earn $50,000 per year, you may need a policy worth $500,000–$750,000 to replace lost income.

2 Debt & Financial Obligations

- Mortgage balance, credit card debt, car loans, and student loans should all be covered.
- Example: If you owe $200,000 on your mortgage, your policy should cover that amount so your family can stay in their home.

3 Future Expenses & Goals

- Will your spouse need additional income?
- Do you plan to fund college tuition for your children?
- Will there be medical or long-term care expenses for elderly dependents?

Section 3: The DIME Method – A Simple Calculation Formula

A quick way to estimate your coverage needs is the DIME Method:

Factor	Description	Example Calculation
D – Debt	Outstanding loans, mortgage, and final expenses	$250,000 mortgage + $20,000 credit card debt = $270,000
I – Income Replacement	Number of years your family needs support	$60,000 x 10 years = $600,000
M – Mortgage	Ensure your home loan is covered	Already included in debt
E – Education	College tuition for children or dependents	$150,000 per child (x2 children) = $300,000
Total Recommended Coverage	Sum of all categories	$1,170,000

 Using this formula ensures your policy covers all financial responsibilities.

Section 4: Customizing Your Coverage Based on Life Stage

Your coverage needs change over time. Here's how to adjust your policy based on where you are in life:

 ### Young Professionals & Students

- Lower coverage is needed if you have no dependents.
- Consider a short-term policy to lock in low premiums.

 ### Families with Children

- High coverage needs due to income replacement, mortgage, and education costs.
- Term or permanent life insurance can provide long-term protection.

 ### Homeowners & Married Couples

- Coverage should match the mortgage balance and household income needs.
- A joint policy for spouses may be an option.

 ### Retirees & Empty Nesters

- Less coverage may be enough if debts are paid and kids are independent.
- Some opt for final expense insurance to cover funeral costs and estate taxes.

Life insurance isn't one-size-fits-all. Your needs evolve with life events, such as marriage, having children, homeownership, or retirement.

Section 5: Choosing the Right Policy Amount

Here's how to match coverage with your financial goals:

Coverage Amount	Best For
$50,000 – $100,000	Covering funeral expenses & small debts
$250,000 – $500,000	Income replacement & mortgage protection
$1M+	Large family needs, estate planning & wealth transfer

Final Thoughts: Ensuring You Have Enough Coverage

The right life insurance policy should:

- Cover debts, final expenses, and income replacement.
- Support your family's future financial goals.
- Fit within your budget without overpaying for unnecessary coverage.

In the next chapter, we'll explore policy riders and add-ons that can enhance your coverage to fit your specific needs.

Chapter 5: Understanding Policy Riders and Add-Ons

A life insurance policy can be customized to fit your unique needs using policy riders, optional add-ons that enhance coverage. While riders increase premium costs, they provide additional benefits that can be critical in times of need.

This chapter will explore common riders, how they work, and whether they're worth adding to your policy.

Section 1: What Are Policy Riders?

A policy rider is an optional feature that extends or modifies your life insurance coverage. Some riders provide financial protection while you're still alive, while others enhance the death benefit for your beneficiaries.

- Some riders are free, while others require additional premium payments.
- Not all insurers offer the same riders, so it's essential to compare options.

Riders should align with your needs. You should only pay for extras that provide real value.

Section 2: Common Life Insurance Riders & Their Benefits

Here are some of the most valuable policy riders and how they work:

1. <u>Accidental Death and Dismemberment (AD&D) Rider</u>

- Pays an extra death benefit if you die due to an accident.
- Covers partial payouts if you lose a limb or eyesight or suffer severe injuries.

Best suited for: Individuals with high-risk jobs or those who frequently travel.

2. <u>Disability Waiver of Premium Rider</u>

- Waives future premium payments if you become disabled and unable to work.
- Keeps your policy active without a financial burden.

Best for: Workers who rely on their income to pay insurance premiums.

3 <u>Critical Illness or Chronic Illness Rider</u>

- Provides a lump sum payout if you are diagnosed with a serious illness (cancer, heart disease, stroke, etc.).
- Helps cover medical costs, lost wages, and living expenses.

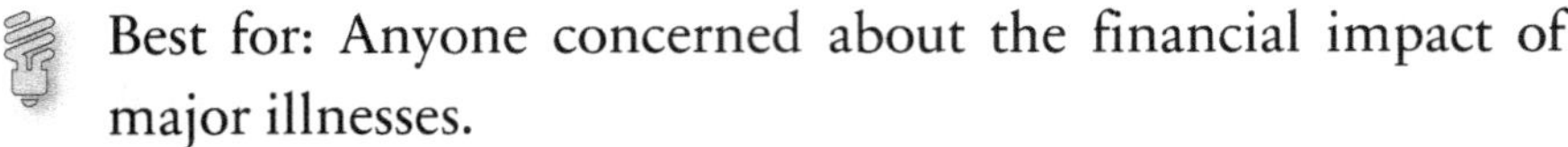

Best for: Anyone concerned about the financial impact of major illnesses.

4 <u>Long-Term Care (LTC) Rider</u>

- Allows you to use part of your death benefit while alive to pay for long-term care (nursing home, assisted living, home healthcare).
- It helps to prevent depleting savings for medical expenses.

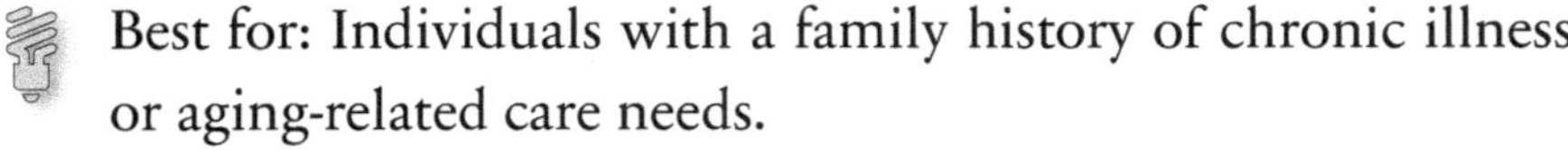

Best for: Individuals with a family history of chronic illness or aging-related care needs.

5 <u>Parent or Child Term Rider</u>

- Adds coverage for children or parents under your policy.
- Provides a small payout in case of their passing, helping with final expenses.

Best for: Parents or individuals financially responsible for aging parents.

6 <u>**Return of Premium (ROP) Rider**</u>

- Refunds all premiums paid if you outlive your term life insurance policy.
- More expensive than regular term insurance, but provides a savings feature.

Best for: Those who want coverage but don't want to "lose money" if they outlive the policy.

Section 3: Comparing Riders – Which Ones Are Worth It?

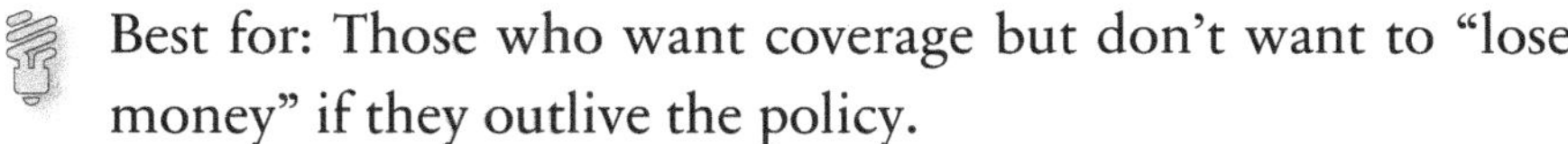

Rider	Benefit	Best For	Worth the Extra Cost?
Accidental Death (AD&D)	Extra payout if death is accident-related	High-risk jobs, travelers	If high risk
Disability Waiver	Premiums waived if disabled	Sole income earners	Highly recommended
Critical Illness	Cash payout for medical costs	Those with a family medical history	If concerned about a major illness
Long-Term Care	Covers nursing/home care costs	Middle-aged & seniors	If no separate LTC plan

Child/Parent Term	Covers children/parents	Families	Optional, depending on need
Return of Premium (ROP)	Refund premiums if no claim	Those who dislike losing money on term policies	Expensive but appealing

 Choose riders based on your personal risk factors, budget, and financial priorities.

Section 4: How to Add Riders to Your Policy

Most riders must be added at the time of policy purchase, but some can be added later. Here's how:

- Review options with your insurer – Not all companies offer the same riders.
- Consider your future needs – Some riders are more valuable as you age.
- Weigh the cost vs. benefit – A rider can be worth the extra protection if the additional premium is negligible.

 Some riders expire when you reach a certain age, so read the fine print!

Final Thoughts: Customizing Your Policy for Maximum Benefit

Policy riders allow you to tailor your life insurance policy to meet specific needs, whether protecting against disability, major illness, or long-term care costs.

- Not all riders are necessary for everyone, but some can be life-saving in the right situations.
- When choosing riders, focus on what aligns with your financial and family situation.

In the next chapter, we'll explore how life insurance can be used as a wealth-building tool, including cash value accumulation and investment options.

Chapter 6: Life Insurance as a Wealth-Building Tool

Life insurance isn't just about protecting your family after you're gone; it can also be a powerful financial tool while you're alive. Permanent life insurance policies, in particular, offer cash value accumulation, tax advantages, and investment opportunities that can enhance your long-term wealth strategy.

In this chapter, we will explore how life insurance can be leveraged to grow wealth, supplement retirement income, and facilitate effective estate planning.

Section 1: Understanding Cash Value in Life Insurance

What Is Cash Value?

Cash value is a savings component that grows within permanent life insurance policies, functioning like an investment account within your policy that accumulates over time.

- A portion of your premium is deposited into this account and grows tax-deferred.
- You can borrow against it, withdraw from it, or use it to pay premiums.

Whole life, universal life, and variable life insurance all have cash value components.

Unlike term life insurance, which has no cash value, permanent life insurance provides protection and financial assets.

Section 2: Ways to Use Life Insurance as a Wealth-Building Tool

1 <u>Borrowing Against Your Policy</u>

- You can take a loan from your cash value without going through a bank.
- There are no credit checks, and interest rates are lower than traditional loans.
- If unpaid, the loan amount is deducted from the death benefit.

Best for: Emergency funds, business capital, or real estate investment.

2 <u>Using Cash Value for Retirement Income</u>

- You can withdraw cash or take out policy loans to supplement your retirement income.
- Withdrawals may be tax-free up to the amount you've paid in premiums.

- Helps bridge income gaps without relying solely on pensions or investments.

💡 Best suited for: Individuals seeking an additional retirement income stream.

3 <u>Tax Advantages of Cash Value Policies</u>

- Tax-Deferred Growth – Cash value grows without immediate taxation.
- Tax-Free Death Benefit – Beneficiaries receive a lump sum payout without taxes (in most cases).
- Tax-Free Loans & Withdrawals – If structured properly, you can access cash value without triggering taxes.

💡 Best suited for: Individuals seeking tax-efficient wealth accumulation.

Section 3: Using Life Insurance for Estate Planning

Life insurance plays a crucial role in passing wealth to heirs efficiently.

1 <u>Covering Estate Taxes & Inheritance Costs</u>

- If your estate is large, heirs may owe estate or inheritance taxes.

- Life insurance provides immediate liquidity to cover these costs without selling assets.

 Best for: High-net-worth individuals and property owners.

2 Irrevocable Life Insurance Trusts (ILITs)

- You can place a life insurance policy in a trust to shield it from estate taxes.
- Ensures the death benefit is used as intended (e.g., distributed over time, protected from creditors).

 Best for: Those who want control over how their heirs receive the payout.

Section 4: Life Insurance for High-Net-Worth Individuals

Wealthy individuals often utilize life insurance to preserve their assets, minimize taxes, and maintain financial flexibility.

1 Premium Financing – Borrowing to Pay for Policies

- Instead of using personal funds, some buy large life insurance policies using loans.
- The death benefit repays the loan, creating net wealth growth.

 2 <u>Business & Estate Protection Strategies</u>

- Used in buy-sell agreements for business continuity.
- Funds charitable giving while offering tax deductions.

Best for: Business owners, investors, and estate planners.

Section 5: When Does Life Insurance as an Investment Make Sense?

Scenario	Is Life Insurance a Good Investment?	
Need basic income replacement?	☒	Term life is a better, cheaper option
Looking for tax-advantaged savings?	☑	Permanent life insurance can help
Want access to cash while alive?	☑	Yes, if you need financial flexibility
High net worth & estate planning?	☑	Ideal for wealth transfer strategies

 If your main goal is pure investment, other vehicles (stocks, IRAs, real estate) may offer better returns. But life insurance provides stability, tax benefits, and liquidity advantages.

Final Thoughts: Making Life Insurance Work for You

Life insurance can be a multi-purpose financial tool beyond just a safety net. When used strategically, it offers:

- A secure way to build wealth with tax advantages.
- A flexible financial safety net through policy loans and withdrawals.
- An innovative estate planning strategy to pass down wealth efficiently.

The next chapter will explore how business owners can utilize life insurance to safeguard and expand their enterprises.

Chapter 7: Business and Life Insurance

Life insurance isn't just for individuals and families; it's also a critical tool for business owners, entrepreneurs, and company executives. Whether you're protecting your business from financial risks, securing funding, or ensuring smooth ownership transitions, life insurance can be a key component of a long-term business strategy.

This chapter will explore how life insurance benefits business owners, including buy-sell agreements, key person insurance, and business loan protection.

Section 1: Why Business Owners Need Life Insurance

If you own a business, you likely have financial obligations that extend beyond your personal life. Life insurance can protect against risks such as:

- Loss of a key employee or partner – If a vital member of your business dies, life insurance can provide financial stability.

- Debt repayment – Many business owners take on loans; a policy ensures debts don't fall on family or partners.

⬡ Ownership transfer – Ensures a smooth transition of business ownership.

⬡ Employee benefits – Offering life insurance can attract and retain top talent.

💡 Life insurance helps businesses remain financially secure even in unpredictable situations.

Section 2: Buy-Sell Agreements – Protecting Business Ownership

A buy-sell agreement ensures that if a business owner or partner dies, their shares can be bought by the remaining owners rather than falling into unintended hands (e.g., heirs who don't want to run the business).

How It Works

1. Business owners take out life insurance policies on each other.

2. If one partner dies, the policy payout is used to purchase their shares.

3. The business remains financially stable and in the right hands.

Types of Buy-Sell Agreements

Agreement Type	How It Works	Best For
Cross-Purchase	Each owner buys a policy on the other owners	Small businesses with few owners
Entity Purchase	The company has policies for all owners and buys shares if one dies	Larger businesses with multiple stakeholders

 A properly structured buy-sell agreement ensures a smooth business transition and financial protection. Legal assistance is usually recommended when drafting these agreements, as legislation may vary in different territories.

Section 3: Key Person Insurance – Protecting Against the Loss of Essential Employees

Some employees are so vital to a company's success that their unexpected death could cause significant financial losses. Key person insurance protects the company by providing funds to:

- Cover lost revenue from the key person's absence.
- Hire and train a replacement.
- Reassure investors and stakeholders of business continuity.

 Best suited for: CEOs, top executives, founders, lead salespeople, or any employee whose loss would have a significant financial impact on the company.

Section 4: Using Life Insurance for Business Loan Protection

Many small businesses take out loans to fund operations or expansion. Lenders often require a life insurance policy as collateral, ensuring repayment if the borrower dies.

- Loan Collateral Insurance – Business owners take out a life insurance policy equal to the amount of the loan.
- If the owner passes away, the policy payout covers the outstanding debt.
- It protects family members and partners from being burdened by unpaid loans.

 Best suited for: startups, business owners with high debt, or companies that rely heavily on a single key individual for financial stability.

Section 5: Group Life Insurance – Employee Benefits That Attract Talent

Offering life insurance as part of your employee benefits package can improve recruitment, retention, and morale.

<u>Group Life Insurance vs. Individual Life Insurance</u>

Feature	Group Life Insurance	Individual Life Insurance
Who owns the policy?	Employer	Employee
Who pays the premium?	Employer (or shared cost)	Employee
Coverage amount	Usually lower (e.g., 1–2x salary)	Flexible, based on needs
Portable?	No, ends when employment ends	Yes, stays with the individual

 Offering group life insurance helps businesses remain competitive in attracting top talent.

Final Thoughts: Using Life Insurance as a Business Strategy

Life insurance is more than just protection; it's a strategic business tool that can:

- Ensure ownership transitions go smoothly.

- Provide financial security in case of a key person's death.

- Protect against business loan liabilities.

- Improve employee retention with group benefits.

In the next chapter, we'll explore life insurance and family stewardship.

Chapter 8: Life Insurance and Family Stewardship

Life insurance does more than protect financial assets; it reinforces the values of responsibility, foresight, and care that define true family stewardship. At its core, stewardship means managing resources wisely, not just for one's benefit, but for the good of future generations. Life insurance plays a key role in this philosophy by ensuring continuity, easing transitions, and encouraging open conversations about money, legacy, and purpose.

Section 1: Stewardship Begins with Planning

Family stewardship starts with recognizing that the decisions made today shape tomorrow's opportunities. Life insurance helps create a safety net that can absorb financial shocks, such as the sudden loss of income, education funding needs, or end-of-life expenses. But its deeper purpose lies in providing a stable foundation on which families can build, dream, and thrive.

A well-structured policy is an expression of care and foresight, reflecting the policyholder's commitment to those they love and demonstrating that their well-being is protected even in the face of uncertainty.

Fostering Open Family Conversations

One of the most overlooked benefits of life insurance is its ability to prompt meaningful family discussions. Many families avoid discussing money, death, or future plans, yet these conversations are essential for true stewardship. Life insurance can serve as a neutral starting point for these talks.

Topics might include:
- Who will be responsible for managing the estate or trust?
- Are there special needs or circumstances for family members?
- How should the benefits be used: education, caregiving, homeownership?

Bringing these topics to light not only ensures smoother transitions but also gives family members a voice in shaping the legacy they are building.

Preparing Heirs for Inheritance

Leaving behind a significant life insurance benefit is generous, but without preparation, it can also be overwhelming. Stewardship involves helping heirs understand financial responsibility, setting goals, and the values that guided the gift. This may involve:

- Encouraging financial literacy for younger generations.
- Writing a legacy letter explaining the intentions behind the policy.
- Working with financial advisors to coach beneficiaries.

The aim is to ensure the inheritance enriches lives, rather than derails them.

Section 2: Supporting Caregiving and Multi-Generational Roles

Family stewardship often includes supporting multiple generations, elderly parents, children, and sometimes grandchildren. Life insurance can provide funding to:

- Cover long-term care needs.
- Pay for a dependent's future care.
- Replace lost income for a primary caregiver.

By addressing these roles, the policy becomes more than a lump-sum benefit; it becomes a tool of compassion and continuity.

From Transaction to Tradition

When life insurance is viewed only as a financial transaction, its potential is limited. However, when integrated into a family's larger story, it becomes a tradition: a practice of responsible, loving leadership passed down over time. Children who witness their parents' planning are more likely to adopt the same mindset, creating a culture of stewardship.

Encouraging Stewardship Over Entitlement

One concern many policyholders share is the fear of creating entitlement rather than gratitude. This is where intentional design and communication are crucial. Rather than simply naming a beneficiary, some choose to use trusts, staggered payouts, or charitable components to instill purpose and perspective.

The message becomes: This isn't just a gift, it's a responsibility.

Final Thoughts: Life Insurance And Family Stewardship

Life insurance is a mirror of your values. It's not only about protecting wealth, but also about passing along wisdom, structure, and stability. In the hands of a thoughtful steward, a life insurance policy becomes a legacy blueprint, offering not just a payout but a promise.

In the next chapter, we'll explore protecting loved ones with special needs.

Chapter 9: Protecting Loved Ones with Special Needs

For families who care for a loved one with special needs, life insurance can be more than a financial tool; it can be a safeguard for a lifetime of care. Planning for the long-term well-being of someone with a disability requires careful coordination of legal, financial, and emotional factors. Life insurance offers a unique way to ensure that your loved one is supported, even when you're no longer there to provide that care yourself.

Section 1: The Unique Planning Challenges

Unlike typical dependents who may become financially independent over time, individuals with special needs often require lifelong support. This support may involve:

- Ongoing medical care.
- Daily living assistance.
- Therapy, equipment, or specialized education.
- Housing arrangements and supervised care.

The cost of such care over a lifetime can be significant. While government programs like Supplemental Security Income (SSI) and Medicaid may help, they have strict asset and income limits. A direct inheritance from a life insurance policy could unintentionally disqualify your loved one from receiving these essential benefits.

Life Insurance as a Funding Solution

A properly structured life insurance policy can provide the funds needed to support a loved one with special needs, without compromising their access to government programs. The key lies in determining where the policy benefit is allocated.

Establishing a Special Needs Trust

Rather than naming the individual as the policy's beneficiary, families often set up a special needs trust (also known as a supplemental needs trust). This trust:

- Holds assets for the benefit of the individual.
- It is managed by a trustee (a person or institution) who makes distributions.
- Allows the beneficiary to remain eligible for public assistance programs.

A life insurance policy can be designed to fund this trust upon the policyholder's death, resulting in a reliable and protected source of financial support tailored to the individual's long-term needs.

Section 2: Choosing the Right Policy

Because this is a long-term plan, permanent life insurance is generally recommended. It ensures that coverage is in place regardless of how long the policyholder lives. Key considerations include:

- Choosing a policy with a guaranteed death benefit.
- Ensuring premiums are affordable over time.
- Considering survivorship policies for couples.

Some families use second-to-die policies (also called survivorship insurance), which pay out after both parents pass away, making them ideal for funding special needs trusts at a time when both primary caregivers are gone.

Coordinating with Estate Planning

Life insurance and special needs planning should be integrated into a comprehensive estate plan. This may involve:

- Naming the special needs trust as the policy beneficiary.
- Appointing a responsible and informed trustee.
- Including guardianship plans or letters of intent.
- Reviewing and updating the plan as laws and circumstances change.

Example:

Consider a couple with a son who has a developmental disability and will require support throughout his life. They create a special needs trust and purchase a whole life policy that names the trust as the beneficiary. Upon their deaths, the policy pays out to the trust, ensuring their son has access to care, housing, and meaningful activities, without disrupting his public benefits.

Working with Professionals

Due to the complexity of these arrangements, it's crucial to work with experienced professionals:

- An attorney who practices in this area of law.
- Financial advisors are familiar with disability planning.
- Trust administrators or fiduciaries.

This team ensures that your good intentions translate into effective and lasting results.

Final Thoughts: Using Life Insurance As Protection For Loved Ones With Special Needs

Every parent or caregiver wants to know that their loved one will be safe, cared for, and treated with dignity even after they're gone. Life insurance, when paired with thoughtful planning, provides peace of mind that this legacy of love and protection will endure. In this way, your policy becomes more than a benefit; it becomes a bridge to a secure and supported future.

In the next chapter, we'll explore philanthropy through life insurance.

Chapter 10: Philanthropy Through Life Insurance

For those who seek to make a lasting impact beyond their family, life insurance offers a powerful and often underutilized tool for philanthropy. Whether you're passionate about education, faith-based missions, health causes, or community development, life insurance can amplify your giving potential in ways that are both meaningful and strategic.

Section 1: Why Use Life Insurance for Charitable Giving?

Life insurance allows individuals to make larger charitable gifts than they might otherwise afford during their lifetime. By leveraging relatively modest premium payments into significant future payouts, donors can create enduring legacies that align with their values and aspirations.

Benefits include:

- The ability to leave a substantial gift without reducing current assets.
- Possible tax advantages (depending on jurisdiction).
- Flexibility in structuring charitable intent.
- Ensuring that philanthropic goals are fulfilled even if life is cut short.

Section 2: Methods of Giving Through Life Insurance

There are several ways to structure a philanthropic gift using life insurance:

1 Naming a Charity as the Beneficiary

The simplest approach is to designate a nonprofit organization as the beneficiary of an existing or new policy. Upon death, the charity receives the proceeds. This option requires no change in policy ownership and can often be done through a simple update to the beneficiary form.

2 Donating a Policy Directly to a Charity

In this method, the donor transfers ownership of a life insurance policy to a charitable organization, which may also assume responsibility for premium payments. If the policy has cash value, the donor may receive an immediate tax deduction for the policy's fair market value.

3 Purchasing a Policy Specifically for Giving

Some individuals purchase a new policy solely for philanthropic purposes. The donor may pay the premiums, while the charity is listed as the owner and beneficiary, securing a guaranteed future gift.

4 Using Life Insurance to Replace Donated Assets

Life insurance can also be used in conjunction with other charitable giving strategies. For example, a donor may give a large asset to charity during their lifetime (such as property or securities) and use a life insurance policy to "replace" that asset for their heirs.

Example: Funding a Scholarship Fund

Consider a retired couple passionate about education. They purchase a permanent life insurance policy, naming their alma mater as the beneficiary. Upon their passing, the policy proceeds establish a named scholarship fund in their honor, benefiting future students for generations.

Integrating with Donor-Advised Funds or Foundations

Life insurance can also be directed to donor-advised funds (DAFs) or private foundations, allowing families to retain some influence over how the funds are distributed over time and enabling a multi-generational approach to philanthropy.

Tax Implications and Considerations

Depending on local tax laws, gifting life insurance can result in:
- Income tax deductions (when donating ownership).
- Estate tax reductions (when removing the death benefit from the taxable estate).
- Gift tax implications (if transferring a policy to a charity).

It's essential to consult with legal and tax advisors to ensure optimal structuring.

Leaving a Legacy That Reflects Your Values

Ultimately, using life insurance for charitable purposes is about aligning financial tools with personal convictions, turning a policy into a mission. Whether your goal is to fund a church, hospital, shelter, or scholarship, your legacy becomes more than what you leave; it becomes what you enable.

Final Thoughts: Philanthropy Through Life Insurance

Philanthropy through life insurance transforms giving from a moment into a movement. It's a way to leave the world better than you found it, ensuring that your impact endures long after you're gone. With proper planning, your generosity can echo through generations and positively impact the lives of those you'll never meet, yet forever affect.

In the next chapter, we'll explore life insurance and blended families: navigating complex relationships.

Chapter 11: Life Insurance and Blended Families: Navigating Complex Relationships

Blended families, those that include children, stepchildren, and spouses from previous relationships, are increasingly common. While they bring new beginnings, they also introduce complex financial and emotional dynamics. Life insurance can play a key role in supporting harmony and protecting loved ones if it's structured thoughtfully.

This chapter explores how life insurance can serve as a stabilizing force in blended families, helping to manage competing priorities, clarify intentions, and reduce the risk of future conflict.

Section 1: The Planning Challenges of Blended Families

In traditional families, deciding how to divide life insurance benefits may be relatively straightforward. In blended families, however, questions arise like:

- How do I ensure children from a prior marriage are provided for?
- What if my new spouse and my adult children have different needs or expectations?
- How can I prevent disputes or feelings of favoritism?

These are difficult but essential questions. A well-structured life insurance plan provides clarity and fairness while respecting the emotional complexity of the family structure.

Clear Beneficiary Designations Matter

One of the most important actions you can take is clearly naming beneficiaries. Relying on assumptions, like thinking your spouse will "do the right thing" and share the benefit, is risky and often leads to disputes.

With blended families, consider:
- Naming specific individuals rather than "my children" (which may cause legal ambiguity).
- Designating multiple beneficiaries with exact percentages.
- Reviewing beneficiary designations after major life events (e.g., remarriage, birth of a child).

It's also wise to update old policies to reflect your current wishes. Otherwise, an ex-spouse could still be legally entitled to receive the benefit.

Using Life Insurance to Equalize Inheritance

Life insurance can be used to "balance" inheritances when other assets, such as a family home or business, are earmarked for specific heirs. For example:

- You leave your house to your new spouse, but use a life insurance policy to provide an equal-value benefit to your children from a prior marriage.
- You pass your business to a child who works in it, but provide a death benefit to other children to maintain fairness.

This strategy reduces resentment and gives you control over how your legacy is shared.

Creating Trusts for Control and Protection

Trusts are especially useful in blended family planning, as they allow you to direct how and when funds are distributed, thereby protecting all parties from miscommunication or misuse.

Options include:

- A revocable living trust that holds the life insurance benefit for your spouse during their lifetime, with the remainder going to your children.
- A testamentary trust is triggered upon your death, controlling the disbursement schedule for minor or adult children.
- A marital trust that supports your spouse while ensuring remaining assets go to your biological children.

By naming the trust, not individuals, as the beneficiary, you gain greater control and minimize potential disputes.

Section 2: Communicate Your Intentions

Money can stir up deep emotions, especially when grief and blended loyalties are involved. One of the best protections you can offer is transparency. Consider:

- Holding family meetings to explain your wishes (or do so in writing).
- Leaving a legacy letter to share your values and reasoning.
- Working with a neutral advisor or estate attorney to guide the conversation.

When your intentions are clearly stated and documented, it reduces the likelihood of misunderstandings or litigation.

Example:

If a man in his sixties remarries and wants to provide for his new wife while also leaving a legacy to his children from a previous marriage, it is recommended that he set up a permanent life insurance policy naming his children as beneficiaries, while leaving other assets, such as his pension and home, to his wife. This clear, deliberate plan avoids tension and ensures both sides of the family feel respected.

Final Thoughts: Using Life Insurance To Navigate Complex Relationships In Blended Families

Blended families require blended planning that is sensitive, inclusive, and strategic. Life insurance, when utilized wisely, can honor past commitments while embracing new ones, creating peace rather than confusion, fairness rather than friction, and a legacy of unity rather than division.

In the next chapter, we'll explore common mistakes and how to avoid them.

Chapter 12: Common Mistakes and How to Avoid Them

Buying life insurance is one of the most important financial decisions you'll make. However, many people make costly mistakes that leave them underinsured, overpaying, or with policies that don't meet their needs.

This chapter will cover the most common life insurance mistakes and how to avoid them so you can make a wise, informed decision.

Section 1: Underestimating How Much Coverage You Need

Many people buy too little coverage, assuming their savings or employer-provided life insurance will be enough. However, they often fail to account for:

- ☒ Future expenses (children's education, spouse's retirement).
- ☒ Inflation reduces the value of their coverage over time.
- ☒ Debts and financial obligations that won't disappear after their passing.

 ### <u>Avoiding the Mistake:</u>

- Use the income replacement rule (10–15 times your annual income).
- Calculate coverage based on debts, expenses, and financial goals.
- Don't rely on employer-provided insurance alone; it usually isn't enough.

Section 2: Buying the Wrong Type of Life Insurance

Some people purchase permanent life insurance when they only need term coverage, while others opt for term insurance when they could benefit from cash value accumulation.

Mistake	What Happens?	Better Approach
Buying term when you need lifelong coverage	Policy expires, leaving you uninsured later in life	Consider permanent insurance for lifelong needs
Buying permanent when you only need temporary coverage	Overpaying for unnecessary benefits	Term insurance is more affordable for short-term needs
Not reviewing policy options	Missing better features or lower premiums	Compare different policy types before deciding

 **<u>Avoiding the Mistake:</u>**

- Choose term life insurance if you only need coverage for a specific period (e.g., mortgage, children's education).
- Choose permanent life insurance if you need lifetime coverage, estate planning, or wealth-building features.
- Work with an insurance professional to compare policies before buying.

Section 3: Waiting Too Long to Buy Coverage

Life insurance premiums are based on age and health; the longer you wait, the more expensive it becomes.

Age	Estimated Monthly Premium for a 20-Year Term ($500,000 Coverage)
25 Years Old	$20–$30
35 Years Old	$30–$40
45 Years Old	$60–$90
55 Years Old	$120–$180

 **<u>Avoiding the Mistake:</u>**

- Buy life insurance as early as possible to lock in low rates.

- Even if you're young and healthy, don't assume you'll always qualify for the same rates.
- Consider convertible term policies if you want flexibility later.

Section 4: Naming the Wrong Beneficiary (or Forgetting to Update It)

Many people fail to update their beneficiaries, which can lead to legal disputes, unintended payouts, or financial complications.

<u>Common Beneficiary Mistakes:</u>

- ☒ Naming a minor child without setting up a trust (minors can't directly receive payouts).
- ☒ Keeping an ex-spouse as the beneficiary after divorce.
- ☒ Forgetting to update beneficiaries after major life events (marriage, birth of a child, etc.).

<u>Avoiding the Mistake:</u>

- Review and update your beneficiaries every few years or after significant life changes.
- If naming a child, set up a trust so a guardian can manage the funds.
- List primary and contingent beneficiaries to ensure the payout goes where intended.

Section 5: Letting Your Policy Lapse

Missing premium payments can cause your policy to lapse, resulting in the loss of coverage and potentially requiring you to reapply at higher rates.

Why Policies Lapse	Impact
Missed payments	Coverage is canceled
Financial struggles	Risk of leaving the family unprotected
Forgetting about the policy	No payout for beneficiaries

 **<u>Avoiding the Mistake:</u>**

- Set up automatic payments to ensure you never miss a premium.
- Choose a policy with a grace period (most give 30 days to catch up on payments).
- If struggling financially, explore policy loans or cash value options (for permanent policies).

Section 6: Relying Only on Employer-Provided Life Insurance

Many people assume their employer's life insurance is enough, but most workplace policies provide only 1–2 times your salary, far less than the recommended 10–15 times your income.

- Employer-provided coverage ends when you leave the job.
- Coverage limits may not fully protect your family.
- You may be unable to move with your insurance policy to another employer.

In some cases, a conversion privilege may be exercised within thirty days, or the employer coverage will expire.

Avoiding the Mistake:

- Treat employer-provided insurance as a supplement, not your primary coverage.
- Get an individual policy to ensure coverage continues even if you change jobs.
- Compare coverage amounts and fill in the gaps with personal insurance.

Final Thoughts: Getting Life Insurance Right

Avoiding these common mistakes ensures you:

- Have the right amount of coverage to protect your loved ones.
- Choose the best policy type for your needs.
- Keep your policy active and up to date.

In the next chapter, we'll discuss how the claims process works and what beneficiaries should know when filing a claim.

Chapter 13: The Claims Process and Payouts

Life insurance provides financial security, but beneficiaries must know how to file a claim to receive the death benefit. Understanding the claims process can help avoid delays, denials, or disputes when a loved one passes away.

This chapter will explore the process of filing a claim, payout options, and what to do if a claim is denied.

Section 1: How to File a Life Insurance Claim

Beneficiaries must file a claim to receive the death benefit payout upon the policyholder's death.

Step-by-Step Guide to Filing a Claim

1 **Locate the Policy Information**

- Find the life insurance policy or contact the insurance company.
- Determine the policy number, coverage amount, and named beneficiaries.

② Gather Required Documents

- A certified copy of the death certificate (needed for all claims).
- A completed claim form from the insurance provider.
- Any supporting documents (e.g., medical records, proof of identity).

③ Submit the Claim

- Contact the insurance company (by phone, online, or in person).
- Provide all required documents to initiate claim processing.

④ Wait for Processing & Approval

- The insurer reviews the claim (typically within 2–4 weeks).
- If everything is in order, the claim is approved, and payment is made.

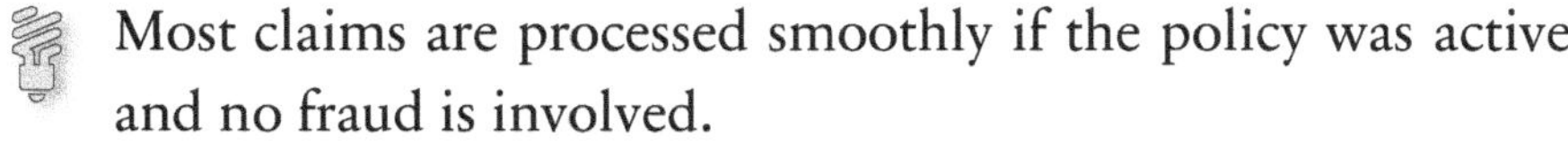

Most claims are processed smoothly if the policy was active and no fraud is involved.

Section 2: Understanding Life Insurance Payout Options

Beneficiaries can choose how they receive the death benefit, depending on their financial needs.

① <u>**Lump Sum Payment (Most Common)**</u>

- The full amount is paid at once.
- Best for: Paying off debts, mortgages, and large expenses.

② <u>**Installment Payouts**</u>

- The benefit is divided into monthly or annual payments.
- Best for: Providing long-term financial support for dependents.

③ <u>**Retained Asset Account**</u>

- The insurer holds the payout in an interest-bearing account.
- Beneficiaries can withdraw funds as needed.
- Best for: Those who want access to funds without managing a large sum at once.

Choosing the right payout option depends on your financial goals and spending habits.

Section 3: Why Life Insurance Claims Get Denied (and How to Avoid It)

Although most claims are approved, some get denied due to policy violations or missing information.

Reason for Denial	What Happens?	How to Avoid It
Policy Lapse	No payout if the policyholder stopped paying premiums.	Keep payments up to date & set up auto-pay
Contestability Period Issues	If the insured dies within the first 2 years, the insurer may investigate for fraud.	Always provide accurate health and lifestyle information when applying.
Misrepresentation of Information	False medical or financial details can lead to denial.	Be honest on your application to avoid claim disputes.
Suicide Clause	No payout if death is ruled as suicide within the first 1–2 years.	Understand policy exclusions before buying.
Exclusions for Risky Activities	Some policies exclude deaths from dangerous hobbies (e.g., skydiving)	Disclose high-risk activities upfront or get an insurer that covers them.

 Understanding policy exclusions and keeping them active prevents claim denials.

Section 4: What to Do If a Claim Is Denied

If a life insurance claim is denied, beneficiaries can appeal the decision by taking these steps:

- Request a Written Explanation – The insurer must provide a reason for the denial.

- Review the Policy Terms – Ensure the policy was active and the claim was valid.

- Provide Additional Documentation – Medical records, financial statements, or witness statements may help overturn the decision.

- Consult an Attorney or Financial Advisor – A legal expert can help resolve disputes.

- File a Complaint – If needed, file a complaint with the insurance regulatory authority in your country.

A denied claim doesn't always mean the end; many can be overturned with the proper documentation.

Final Thoughts: Preparing Beneficiaries for the Claims Process

To ensure a smooth claims process, policyholders should:

- Inform beneficiaries about the policy details.

- Keep all policy documents accessible.

- Review and update beneficiaries regularly.

By planning, you can ensure your loved ones receive their benefits without delays or complications.

In the next chapter, we'll discuss the future of life insurance, including industry trends and innovations shaping how policies are bought and managed.

Chapter 14: The Future of Life Insurance

Life insurance has existed for centuries, but the industry is constantly evolving. Advancements in technology, personalized policies, and regulatory changes are shaping how people buy and manage life insurance.

In this chapter, we'll explore key trends, innovations, and future challenges that could impact policyholders, insurers, and the industry as a whole.

Section 1: Digital Transformation in Life Insurance

1 AI and Automated Underwriting

- Traditional underwriting takes weeks, but AI-driven systems now process applications in minutes.
- Insurers use big data and predictive analytics to assess risk more accurately.
- Some policies are now instant issue; no medical exam required.

 AI reduces human bias and makes coverage more accessible, especially for younger consumers.

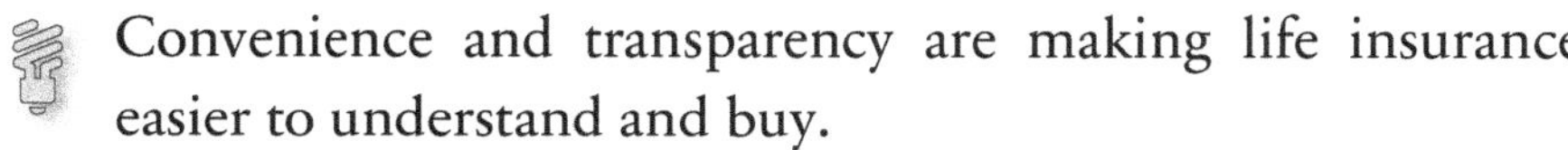

② <u>Online Life Insurance Marketplaces</u>

- Buying life insurance used to require in-person meetings, but now policies can be purchased 100% online.
- Comparison websites allow consumers to shop for the best rates and features in minutes.
- More people prefer digital interactions over traditional agent-based sales.

Convenience and transparency are making life insurance easier to understand and buy.

Section 2: Personalized and Flexible Policies

① <u>On-Demand & Pay-As-You-Go Life Insurance</u>

- Some insurers now offer pay-as-you-go life insurance based on real-time data.
- Premiums adjust based on health, lifestyle, and behavior tracking (e.g., fitness habits).
- This model is gaining popularity among younger, healthier individuals.

 Personalized pricing rewards those who maintain a healthy lifestyle.

2 Hybrid Life Insurance Products

- More policies combine life insurance with investment or retirement features.
- Some offer flexible coverage that adapts to major life events (e.g., marriage, children, retirement).
- Hybrid policies allow people to access cash value benefits while still alive.

 Consumers are looking for policies that evolve with their financial needs.

Section 3: The Impact of Inflation on Life Insurance

1 Rising Costs of Premiums

- Inflation affects life insurance just like any other financial product.
- Higher medical costs and longer life expectancies may drive premium increases.
- Policyholders may need to adjust coverage amounts to maintain real value.

② <u>Inflation-Protected Policies</u>

- Some insurers now offer inflation-adjusted life insurance policies.
- These policies automatically increase coverage over time to keep up with rising costs.

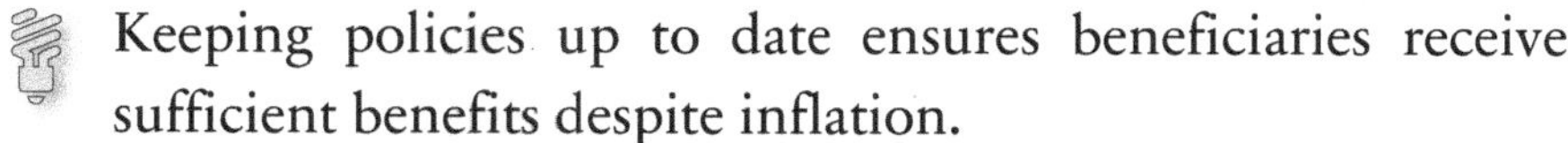 Keeping policies up to date ensures beneficiaries receive sufficient benefits despite inflation.

Section 4: The Role of Blockchain & Smart Contracts

① <u>Fraud Prevention & Transparency</u>

- Blockchain technology provides tamper-proof records of policies and claims.
- It helps to prevent fraud, errors, and disputes over policy terms.

② <u>Faster Claims Processing</u>

- Smart contracts automate payouts upon verification of death certificates.
- This reduces processing time from weeks to days.

 Blockchain is improving efficiency, security, and customer trust in the industry.

Section 5: Regulatory & Market Shifts

1 Stricter Consumer Protection Laws

- Governments are tightening rules on policy disclosures, premium transparency, and fair pricing.
- Insurers must be more transparent about exclusions, costs, and risks.

2 Expansion of Microinsurance

- Microinsurance provides low-cost life insurance to underserved populations.
- This trend is growing in developing countries, where traditional life insurance is less accessible.

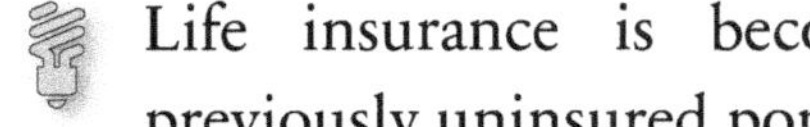 Life insurance is becoming more inclusive, reaching previously uninsured populations.

Final Thoughts: The Future of Life Insurance

The industry is shifting toward greater accessibility, personalization, and efficiency through:

- AI-driven underwriting for faster policy approvals.

- Flexible, hybrid policies that adapt to life changes.

- Blockchain security for fraud prevention and faster claims processing.

- More transparent pricing and consumer protection laws.

The future of life insurance is about making coverage more affordable, efficient, and tailored to individual needs.

What's Next?

Now that you understand how life insurance works, you're equipped to choose the right policy and use it strategically for financial security, wealth-building, and legacy planning.

Thank you for taking this journey through More Than Just A Payout: How Life Insurance Builds Security and Opportunity. May your decisions bring you and your loved ones financial peace of mind.

Sources & Further Reading

To support the information in this book and provide further reading, consider the following reputable sources:

- A.M. Best - www.ambest.com
- American Bar Association. (2020). Estate Planning for Blended Families. Retrieved from https://www.americanbar.org
- Consumer Reports – Insurance - www.consumerreports.org
- Fidelity Investments. (2022). Tips for Estate Planning in a Blended Family. Retrieved from https://www.fidelity.com
- Insurance Information Institute (III) - www.iii.org
- Investopedia – Life Insurance Section - www.investopedia.com
- Leimberg, Stephan R. (2017). The Tools and Techniques of Estate Planning. The National Underwriter Company. LIMRA (Life Insurance Marketing and Research Association). Managing Life Insurance in Complex Family Structures. Retrieved from https://www.limra.com
- National Association of Estate Planners & Councils. (n.d.). Using Trusts in Blended Family Planning. Retrieved from https://www.naepc.org
- National Association of Insurance Commissioners (NAIC) - www.naic.org

- NOLO. (2023). Estate Planning for Blended Families: How to Leave Your Assets Fairly to All Your Loved Ones. Retrieved from https://www.nolo.com

References

The following sources were consulted to ensure accuracy and provide further reading on the topics covered in this book. Readers are encouraged to explore these references for deeper insights into life insurance, financial planning, estate strategies, and business applications.

Academy of Special Needs Planners. (n.d.). Special Needs Answers. Retrieved from https://www.specialneedsanswers.com

American Council of Life Insurers. (2023). 'Life Insurance Fact Book.' Retrieved from https://www.acli.com

American Council of Life Insurers. Life Insurance: A Foundation for Family Financial Security. Retrieved from https://www.acli.com

Feldman, D., & Levine, S. (2022). 'The Financial Advisor's Guide to Life Insurance Planning.' Wiley & Sons.

Hughes Jr., J. E. (2004). Family Wealth: Keeping It in the Family. Bloomberg Press.

Internal Revenue Service. (2023). Publication 526: Charitable Contributions. Retrieved from https://www.irs.gov/forms-pubs/about-publication-526

Kiplinger. (2023). 'Life Insurance Strategies for Wealth Transfer and Tax Planning.' Retrieved from https://www.kiplinger.com

Leave a Legacy. (n.d.). National Association of Charitable Gift Planners. Retrieved from http://www.leavealegacy.org

National Association of Insurance Commissioners. (2023). 'Consumer Guide to Understanding Life Insurance.' Retrieved from https://www.naic.org

Pang, G. (2023). 'Retirement Income and Life Insurance: A Tax-Advantaged Approach.' Journal of Financial Planning, Vol. 36(4), 45-61.

Purposeful Planning Institute. (n.d.). Family Legacy and Stewardship Resources. Retrieved from https://purposefulplanninginstitute.com

Russell, L. Mark, & Grant, Arnold. (2008). Planning for the Future: Providing a Meaningful Life for a Child with a Disability After Your Death (6th ed.). Exceptional Parent Press.

Schwab Charitable. (2021). Using Life Insurance in Charitable Giving. Retrieved from https://www.schwabcharitable.org

Social Security Administration. (2024). Understanding SSI and Resource Limits. Retrieved from https://www.ssa.gov/ssi/text-resources-ussi.htm

Special Needs Alliance. (n.d.). Using Life Insurance in Special Needs Planning. Retrieved from https://www.specialneedsalliance.org

The American College of Financial Services. (n.d.). Philanthropy and Life Insurance: Charitable Planning Strategies. Retrieved from https://www.theamericancollege.edu

T. Rowe Price. (2022). Family Conversations About Money. Retrieved from https://www.troweprice.com

U.S. Securities and Exchange Commission. (2023). 'Variable and Indexed Life Insurance: Investment Considerations.' Retrieved from https://www.sec.gov

Warren, J. (2022). 'Legacy Planning with Life Insurance: Ensuring a Smooth Transfer of Wealth.' Harvard Business Press.

About the Author

Ramoth Watson is a seasoned life insurance professional with **34 years of industry excellence**, spanning three major life insurance companies. With a decade of experience as a **financial advisor** and 24 years as a **sales leader**, he has played a pivotal role in developing the careers of numerous advisors and field managers, leaving a legacy of mentorship and leadership.

Now retired from corporate leadership, Ramoth continues to serve as an **independent financial advisor** with a leading life insurance company in Jamaica. His distinguished career has earned him multiple **prestigious awards**, including the **Million Dollar Round Table (MDRT) Award** and multiple **Agency Manager of the Year** honors, recognizing his outstanding performance and commitment to excellence.

Beyond his professional achievements, Ramoth has been a **key figure in industry education**, moderating the local **industry licensing course** from 2003 to 2024 and the **Financial Services Certified Professional (FSCP) Course** from 2013 to 2018. His dedication to knowledge-sharing has helped shape the next generation of financial professionals.

A leader, mentor, and trusted advisor, Ramoth Watson remains committed to guiding individuals and professionals toward financial security and success.